EZRA H. HEYWOOD

UNCIVIL LIBERTY:

An Essay to Show the Injustice and Impolicy of Ruling Woman Without Her Consent (1873)

Libertarian Broadsides, No. 8

With an Introduction

by

JAMES J. MARTIN

RALPH MYLES PUBLISHER, INC.
COLORADO SPRINGS
1978

International Standard Book Number: 0-87926-023-8

Ralph Myles Publisher, Inc.
P. O. Box 1533
Colorado Springs, Colorado 80901

INTRODUCTION

In reissuing this famous but long-neglected work for the first time in over a century, it is not intended that it furnish a pretext to leap into the complex controversy concerning "women's rights" which has become increasingly intensified in the last fifteen years. The object is rather to bring attention to an undeservedly obscured figure in American intellectual and ideological history, first of all, and to put on the contemporary record one of the overlooked phases of the struggle to achieve equality before the law, especially, for women in the USA.

It has been observed that it has become progressively more difficult to write about any phase of this subject recently, as the language of these times becomes more jagged and hostile, and felicity of expression more and more becomes identified with patronization or condescension. Growing contempt for even the most elementary decencies of politeness and reciprocal civility among far too many, even in public life, has tended to drive from the scene many with something to say, unwilling to brave the blast of contumely and extravagant abuse likely to ensue. An aura of weary futility tends to spread over the entire subject, as it resolves more and more into a combat area reserved for the most intemperate and exaggerated polemic. And the combatants have frequently been various factions of women with one another, and not exclusively women challenging men in the enjoyment of traditional or conventional legalized advantages.

In reality, the so-called "battle of the sexes" has been featured by extensive and continuous fraternization with the enemy on both sides, and periods of active enmity have been matched by eras of cordiality, as well as acts of mutual assistance and cooperation in many worthwhile achievements. And this is so even in matters intellectual, though in some areas the paucity of female contributors has sparked accusations of conspiratorial scheming to deprive them of access.

The American Civil War, like all profound and sweeping cataclysms, unleashed a wide variety of impulses and tendencies involving change. With the end of Negro slavery, the energy once spent in this drive was soon to be channeled to many other causes. The histories of 'reform' list a formidable array of interests which took the place of anti-slavery in the generation roughly after 1865, a much-told story which does not need be recounted once more here. One of these, even over a century ago, was called the "women's rights movement," though it, like many others, had an ancestry which went back well before that time.

There have been certain conventions dealing with the historical narrative which concern this aspect of the country's social history. A well-informed person may become familiar with the life and labors of Susan B. Anthony, Margaret Fuller, the Grimke sisters, Elizabeth Cady Stanton, Lucretia Mott, Dorothea Dix, Frances Willard, perhaps Lucy Stone, and surely Carrie Nation (and spiced probably with a few figures of the likes of Calamity Jane Canary). But it is not likely that this education will include acquaintance with such a brilliant and radical mind as Frances Wright. And while the numerous and sustained efforts to obtain the right to vote may be memorialized, it was not until very recent times that one was likely to be reminded of Victoria Woodhull, who ran for the presidency of the United States on a minority party ticket in 1872, almost 50 years before women were legally eligible to participate in national elections. This act of boldness and daring even now impels 'liberal' proper thinkers to recoil in embarrassment, and to persist in smearing her as a "primitive muckraker" and an unbalanced 'nut.' (Her part in her spirited weekly paper in bringing back down to earth, among the rest of the mortals, the celebrated preacher Henry Ward Beecher, has been detailed in a succession of works.)

Undoubtedly, conventional school histories still overlook very many women whose achievements have merited considerable respect in all quarters. But women are as divided among themselves as to whom they should hold in honor, and their range of attainments is about as wide as that of men. It would seem however that the problem is far from resolved. An example: while women were rejoicing in finally achieving "the vote" and formally entering national politics, who among them made a point of denouncing the gross injustice resulting to Dr. Mary E. Walker from the workings of these same politics at almost that same moment? The second woman to graduate from Syracuse University Medical School and a contract surgeon with the Union Army, she had been the first woman to receive the country's highest military distinction, the Congressional Medal of Honor, in 1866, only to be deprived of this honor fifty years later by an incredible ex post facto law and the workings of an entirely male bureaucratic caper. Here indeed was a 'free spirit' of the first rank, 'notorious' as a 'womens' rights zealot' in her own time, and a victim of one of the most shabby ploys at re-ordering history in the country's entire past, in effect a startling anticipation of the Orwellian "Memory Hole."*

However, the theme motivating this publication event is that of men and women working together to bring about a state of affairs in which arbitrary and artificial barriers crippling the latter are targeted for dissolution. Among the most neglected are the principal figures of individualist anarchism, from Josiah Warren and Stephen Pearl Andrews through the formidable assembly of personalities associated with Benjamin R. Tucker, and after. In the forefront of this group is Ezra H. Heywood, a mercurial personality of first rate intelligence and remarkable eloquence and articulateness. Though his predecessor and latter-day associate, Andrews, that "iceberg of a brain," had a prior reputation for encouraging if not instigating rebellion among women who made his intellectual acquaintance as far back as the 1840s, it was Heywood, beginning in the late 1860s, who became even more formidable (and, probably, more scandalous, in the eyes of the conventional), at stimulating independence and self-expression among those temperamentally so inclined. His remarkable paper, *The Word*, begun in 1872, was anything but a theological sheet, and was open to the writing of women interested in all phases of post-1865 'reform,' including sexual, and its pages were sometimes graced with the blunt and quite startling views on the latter subject of Heywood's wife, the former Angela Tilton.

The Word brought together for the first time some of the writers who later made Tucker's *Liberty* a world-renowned forum. Tucker himself first broke into print in Heywood's paper, and his activities in the 1870s were much influenced by Heywood's "monthly journal of reform." In their respective papers, between 1872 and 1908, Heywood and Tucker gave access to more women contributors than was true of any other two publications anywhere during that time span, quite a few of whom became globally known as a result. These two editors, along with Moses Harman and E. C. Walker, the husband of Harman's daughter, Lillian, who published the smaller contemporary paper, *Lucifer, The Lightbearer*, in Kansas, comprise a long-obscured episode in male cooperation with the women's rights drive in the last quarter of the 19th century, one which is however slowly getting the credit it has long deserved.

This long-delayed issuance of Heywood's 1873 essay, *Uncivil Liberty: An Essay to Show the Injustice and Impolicy of Ruling Women Without Her Consent*, has been done in the effort to acquaint a contemporary audience with some idea of what those of a century ago thought was the primary issue. This was quite likely the most widely circulated undertaking of its kind. The printing from which this new edition is made indicates that it was already at the 60,000 circulation mark, and as it remained available for most of the subsequent 20 years, its full print run surely ran well in excess of this figure. It is not believed anything published by the individualist circle ever exceeded the scope of diffusion of *Uncivil Liberty*.

Heywood's treatise is far from being simply a plea for the extension of the right to vote to women in national elections, though this seemed to be the main matter on the agenda over a century ago. The conviction that American politics would be markedly improved by the adoption of this policy, shared in some circles four and five generations ago, has not been realized, up to now. Women seem to have about the same political wisdom and failings as men; it has been observed with a touch of irony that the first American president for whom women were half-responsible was Warren G. Harding, though in retrospect it might be suggested that none of Harding's successors were known to have pressed Aristotle very much, either. And the latter is true in the case of quite a number of Harding's predecessors as well.

There are several elements in *Uncivil Liberty* which have nothing to do with voting rights and legal equality, and some of them remain unresolved, and probably insoluble, issues. The psycho-social ones appear to some to be far more important, and much less amenable to being dealt with successfully on any but an entirely individual basis for as long into the future as anyone may care to contemplate. Even in a system utterly lacking in legal or psychic intimidation, there will still be the problem of the will to subservience and servitude, regardless of sex.

Uncivil Liberty has some of the flavor of James L. Walker's views on women individually achieving their own emancipation, or 'liberation,' given the will to do so and the temperament to profit from it, as found in the closing sections of Walker's *Philosophy of Egoism*, despite the dissimilar approaches of the two works to the subject. Heywood wrote somewhat more emotionally than Walker, and with more than a touch of the melodramatic sentiment characteristic of the propaganda of the early temperance movement 40 or more years before his time. Despite what has happened in the century since *Uncivil Liberty*, bringing about changes which Heywood and his contemporaries hardly could have even imagined, let alone have predicted (in November, 1978, the world-famous London journal, *The Economist*, listed as No. 1, in its nomination of the ten most important events of the previous 135 years, the vast change in the position and status of women), the subject taken up in that work by Heywood is still immensely significant. Perhaps it is worth a glance backward now, in an effort to appreciate the changes which have taken place, while at the same time recognizing the persistence of a seemingly irreducible element of the problem.

Fall, 1978

JAMES J. MARTIN
Palmer Lake, Colorado

*Dr. Walker was the first woman physician in the world to be commissioned an Army surgeon, and the first woman in history who was exchanged as a prisoner of war for a man of equal rank. She claimed to have been the first woman in U.S. history to attempt to vote at the polls. Dressed in male attire, she was a vigorous suffragette in the U.S. and England from 1866 on.

UNCIVIL LIBERTY

The independence of British American Colonies, asserted in 1776, was an emphatic declaration of the right of peoples to manage their own affairs; an appeal from governments to justice, from men to man. Till then nations were subject to enthroned power, whose will was superior to popular dissent. Singularly enough, the managers of that revolution, after affirming life and liberty to be inalienable rights, proceeded to destroy life by wholesale in battle, and were so insincere as to deny liberty to a weaker race. The same hands which slew tyrants on Bunker Hill spread the shield of Federal law over chattel bondage at the South, and the Union of '89 became "a herd of States hunting slaves." Retributive justice has emancipated and enfranchised black men, but the insincerity of the fathers reappears in the dogma of exclusive male sovereignty, which rules one-half of our adult citizens—the women—against their consent. This rude resistance to the logic of events affronts the essential principles of liberty, which inspired what self-government is yet thought safe in private affairs, and were designed to secure, at least, good manners in rulers.

Human governments originated in force; in the heaviest fist, or with those able to control the mere animal strength of the hour; the exponent of concrete opinion, of what certain men think best to be done, with a large infusion of fraud and violence, it now appears as emperor, president, or pound keeper, set over prone multitudes, until they get on two feet and acknowledge the dominion of principles. Through John Baptist or Herod, Brutus or Cæsar, Cromwell or Stuart, Lincoln or Buchanan, the moral sense, often stifled or perverted, but never conquered, here and there gets into creed, deed, or positive law, and makes the epoch memorable. One evolves a truth and is reviled, starved, or murdered outright for it; the truth survives, overrules law and custom, and men grow famous in eulogizing what they killed the discoverer for announcing. The king's arm being too short to reach the circumference of his realm, he delegates his will to subordinate executors, on whom, in turn, he is somewhat dependent. Thus all governments, in their way, are representative, and rest on consent; though they differ in the width of the circle in the number of nobles taken into royal confidence. But despotism makes the will of monarchy its ultimate appeal, while liberty, accepting as final nothing this side of natural right, defers to popular reason, and is served or cheated, by that democratic king, the average man, the majority. In that marvel to monarchs, a State without a king, all citizens are nobles in so far as they incarnate equity. Hence our fathers, according to their luck, derived just powers of government from consent of the governed; and, to be as good as they, we must be enough better to apply the democratic idea impartially.

In determining essential right we settle woman's rights, for the greater includes the less; every political or reformatory convention is the reappearance of government, through imperfect mediums, the people, from its primary source, natural equity. The subtle law which regulates movements of sovereign particles of the body politic, the cardinal principle of civil liberty allows every one to do what she or he will, provided they invade not the equal right of every other one to do the same. Out of this come freedom of thought, expression and movement; the right of association, habeas corpus, trial by jury, all the safeguards which experience has thrown up around dissent, to withstand invasion, and enable right to give law to intrusive fact. Parties, majorities, state, church—all institutions are despotisms when in conflict with incarnate truth. Legitimate civil authority may be traced to one of two origins: 1st, Enlightened reason, natural equity. 2d, Positive legislation. Since the latter is void unless it enact the former, valid law can have but one source, abstract right, essential truth. Hence government, not less than liberty, must justify its existence, and opponents of impartial suffrage should be classed as tyrants until proved innocent. That this is a correct view some competent exponents of thought, in diffferent ages, may be cited to witness. Socrates: "Whatever inconvenience ensue, nothing is to be preferred before justice." New Testament: "Whether it be right to hearken unto you, more than unto God, judge ye; . . . . . the law is fulfilled in one word, love thy neighbor as thyself." Cicero: "If nature does not ratify law all virtues lose their sway." Bacon: "There are in nature certain fountains of justice, whence all civil laws are derived but as streams." Shakespeare: "In love the heavens themselves do guide the state." Hampden: "What is unjust is not law, and what is not law ought not to be obeyed." Blackstone: "No human laws are of any validity if contrary to the law of nature; and such of them as are valid derive all their force and authority from this original." Kant: "Act so that the immediate motive of your will may become a universal rule for all intelligent beings." Hallam: "God forbid that we should submit our liberties to a jury of antiquaries." Carlyle: "One strong thing I find here below, the just thing, the true thing; if the thing is unjust, thou hast not succeeded." Spooner: "No one can know what the written law is until he knows what it ought to be." Emerson: "Law is only a memorandum; absolute right is the first governor." Lieber: "The forbearing use of power is a sure attribute of a gentleman." The right to rule first claimed by brute force, then by good will, charity, finally rests in liberty, delegated trust, consent. If principal or representative goes wrong, integrity dissents, bides its time and wins, though the true king be in a dungeon, and a culprit on the throne. The world will settle down into a community of peoples when abstract right is obeyed as supreme interpersonal, interstate, international law, and the clearest self-interest.

From this cursory glance at the principles which authorize legitimate government, much now obeyed as law appears destitute of moral justification. An old play represents Adam crossing the stage going to be created; democracy is yet so much in embryo that its reputed statesmen think national unity is promoted by centralized dictation, and extol as "a republican form of government" that which forces the allegiance of dissenting men, and dooms to political servitude all women. But civil law being merely the creature of man, and binding only as it enacts right, those who presume to legislate for citizens—permanent residents of mature age and sound mind, who contribute to the material or moral welfare of society—of either sex or any race without power of attorney, or other definite commission, are guilty of fraudulent usurpation, and their acts morally void. "Taxation without representation is tyranny" was a potent rallying cry in the struggle for a male independence, which compels women to pay for the support of governments they had no voice in creating.* It is a recognized principle of democracy that persons indicted for crime are entitled to be tried by their peers; yet women are arrested, imprisoned and judicially murdered, by their self-constituted masters. By constitutional decree and custom, a majority of votes cast decide the election; in Massachusetts, according to the census of 1865, there are 63,011 more females than males; and, by the majority rule, the women may rightfully expel Legislature and Governor from the State House, as usurpers. Yet these are the fellows who set themselves up as gods, to be petitioned and prayed to, instead of coming down on penitent knees for their transgressions! The validity of the national war debt, the binding force of marriage laws, chartered powers of corporations, title deeds to property, public and private contracts are vitiated by the all-pervading usurpation. Under existing laws only a "prostitute" can claim her child; any married father, whether of age or not, by will or deed may dispose of his child, "born or to be born," and its mother is liable to fines and imprisonment for presuming to dispute his marital "rights." A Boston woman of wealth, culture and talent, allowed a

*An attempt has been made in this State to ascertain the number of females in their respective municipalities who are taxed directly, and also the number of such who have property standing in other people's names. According to these imperfect returns there are 33,961 females in Massachusetts who pay a tax of $1,927,653.11 on a total valuation of $131,683,393.28—*Boston Daily Journal.*

servant to conduct her two little girls, one two and the other five years old, to see their father, then living in another house belonging to her; he immediately took them aboard an Atlantic steamer, carried them to Paris, and she did not see them again for ten years! He acted on legal advice, and the statute which permitted the outrage is still law in most, if not all, of the States. Recently a prominent member of the medical profession compelled his wife to die under his own treatment, rather than be cured, or even prescribed for by the physician of her own choice; and government permits husbands to exercise this murderous power. One unfit to have authority over a fly is made absolute master of his wife; and while he could be arrested for cruelty to a horse in the street, he may enter his house—a castle to him, a prison to her—and whip the mother of his children at pleasure. A just man blushes to look into the statute book, so often does he find himself judged and sentenced by the acts of his sex.

The legal subjection of women is thought to be justified by an assumed natural dependence on man. The old claim of tyranny, "The king can do no wrong," is reasserted by that many-headed monster, the majority, which widens the circle of despotism, but retains the fact. As people were to the king, so woman is now an appendage of man, who claims to be her "head," though nature seems not to have limited heads to the exclusive possession of either sex. That there is no natural feeling of dependence, on one hand, or of superiority on the other, is evident to the most casual observer of spontaneous dealings of the sexes. In practical sense and force a girl of fourteen is often ten years older than a boy of the same age; tells him how to act and protects him from the big boys at school. A widow lady who maintains herself and daughter and lays up money by keeping a half-dozen families in clean clothes, rejoices that she has no man on her hands to support. Her next door neighbor, who sold, one day, forty cents' worth of her husband's service for two pounds of beef, said, that for another piece as large she would part with him entirely. At a court ball in Berlin, Bismarck, much pleased with the wife of a foreign diplomat present, with characteristic audacity, reached out to pluck a flower from the bouquet she carried; rapping his knuckles with her fan she said: "Pardon, Mr. Count, but that flower is not a German State; you must ask for it." Man instinctively defers to woman until poverty, marriage or ungentlemanly arrogance subjects her to his dictation. Popular reverence for her person forbids public laying on of hands to correct her, and private insolence dares not until she is under his legal thumb. She is a stronger body guard to man in a mob than a battalion of soldiers, and the sanctity of her person is the only barrier the savage atrocitites of war never quite overleap. A body, ears, eyes, nose, taste, touch, sensitive to beauty of thought, color, sound; all requisites to admit men to the realm of sense, and a knowledge of material things, woman has; while, in intuition, the income of spiritual wealth, she is admitted to excel man. By what authority, then, is she required to look up to him for guidance, while he looks to Infinite Truth as the source of right and duty? The ruling class rarely yield a privilege until whipped out of it; so man now legislates with his fist rather than his conscience, robs his "better half" of all the ballot, simply because he is physically the strongest. To compel her to obey father before marriage, husband afterward, then her eldest son, may be consistent with Mormonism, which aspires to build an empire on Isaiah's prophecy that in the last days seven women shall cling to one man, and honors as "the wisest man" a patriarch who had seven hundred wives and three hundred concubines; it may be suited to a theology which makes man lord of creation and woman an afterthought, designates boys as the "sons of God" and girls as the "daughters of men," and paves hell, not in good intentions even, but with "infants' skulls not a span long"; it may be agreeable to her position in a Turkish harem, a Chinese palace, on a blazing funeral pile of a Hindoo husband, or in the hotter fires of a Boston brothel, but it is quite repulsive to the free ideas which transformed the dark realms of the American Indian into a constellation of powerful States.

The protesting indignation of some women who had the honor to be, at least, rebellious slaves, widespread and increasing unrest broke out in the first formal declaration of independence, issued in 1848, from Seneca Falls, N. Y., by Elizabeth Cady Stanton, Lucretia Mott, and others. It enumerated grievances equal in number and seriousness to those set down in the famous manifesto of '76, and is destined to work a more extended and beneficent revolution. Current objections to woman's enfranchisement can hardly be accounted for, except on the supposition that the sexes, even husbands and wives, are not yet personally acquainted with each other or truth. Justice unites persons widely remote; injustice separates infinitely those standing side by side. Men reputed to know something of the nature of liberty, so-called radicals who have ceased to represent the moral sense, or even the intelligence of the hour, talk flippantly of "universal suffrage" while shutting out one-half of human-kind. A wit believed in universal salvation, provided he could pick the men; so perhaps these recreant "radicals" will conquer their prejudices against impartial suffrage, when assured the new comers will vote their party ticket. The right of man to political freedom appears in the fact that he is a sentient being, capable of reason and choice, looking before and after. To rule adult citizens against their will is tyranny; women are adult citizens, hence those who deny them the ballot are tyrants. A dozen years ago or more, the writer, with other specimens of sophomoric assurance, one morning at breakfast, questioned the propriety of Lucy Stone's refusal to pay taxes, allowing her furniture to be sold in preference; the combined, college-learned, male wisdom thinking it a great ado about a small matter. A lady opposite, who first called his attention practically to peace and anti-slavery reform, flung over the table, "No taxation without representation. Did you ever hear of Sam. Adams and John Hampden?" It was the first and last argument he ever attempted to make against woman's suffrage. To justify himself, her oppressor must class her psychologically with brutes, deny her a soul, prove either that she has no functions equal with man, or that she is incapable of exercising them—neither of which can be done. Boys who toss their empty heads at this reform, use freely that epithet which reveals so much contempt for the human understanding—"strongminded." Men are thought to personate reason, and women sentiment; but generally male objectors to this claim are noted for nothing more than their plentiful lack of logic and superabundance of mulish prejudice. Notwithstanding these disparaging exceptions, men yield to reason; and, at no distant day, physical strength will rally under the banner of moral beauty.

Whether suffrage is a right or privilege, natural or conventional, its denial to woman is equally indefensible. Minors become of age, slaves are emancipated, lunatics regain reason, idiots are endowed with intelligence, criminals are pardoned, traitors amnestied, disfranchised males of every class shed their disabilities and are restored to liberty; but the fact of sex—the crime of womanhood—dooms one to perpetual vassalage! Not the ability to drink, chew, smoke, lie, steal and swear, votes—though election day too often indicates these vices to be important conditions of membership in the male body politic—but intellect, conscience, character, are supposed to vote; and the boy proudly becoming "a man before his mother," is crowned a sovereign at twenty-one, because in thought and discretion he ceases to crawl as an animal, and stands an upright intelligence. Is she who endowed him with these royal qualities less capable of exercising them? If the admission fee to franchise is not age, but property, why are poor men received and rich women excluded? If the door swings open to integrity and courage, why are these turned away in women while their absence is welcomed in men? Simply because this booted, spurred and whiskered thing called government is a usurpation, and men choose to have it so. Since, then, custom not reason, fraud not justice, prejudice not good sense, object, this is a question not for argument, but for affirmation. Those who acknowledge the validity of existing government, by increasing its numerical power, not merely drop a stitch in their logic, but surrender the flag of impartial suffrage to its enemies. The negro certainly has quite as good a right to vote as his late masters. If ignorant, they made it a penal offence to teach him to read; if poor, they robbed him of his earnings by law. But who are negro men and Chinese that we should confer irresponsible power on them? To admit any man, be he black, red, yellow, or a minor—our curled, white darling just come of age—to the franchise, who is not pledged to share it with women, is treason to liberty, a desertion of the logical duty of the hour.

A cruel kindness, thought to be friendly regard, assumes to "protect" those who, by divine right of rational being, are entitled, at least, to be let alone. We are not among wild beasts; from whom, then, does woman need protection? From her protectors. While making marriage almost her only possible means of permanent subsistence, and working for a living unpopular, custom forbids her to "propose," to seek a husband; hence this vicarious theory of government owes her, what Socrates claimed for himself, a support at the public expense. If in the old law phrase, "the husband and wife are one person, and he that one"; if, married or unmarried, her personality is buried in his, man should also embody her responsibility—be taxed for her food, clothing, leisure, pleasure, and punished for her sins. But, in practice, he does not recognize this obliging doctrine; for, while reserving the hottest corner of his future hell for her, in this life his responsibility ends with the gratification of his personal desires, and she is "abandoned"—thrown upon the tender mercies of public censure and charity. If there is hanging to be done, it is her head which goes through the noose; if imprisonment is decreed her body is locked up; if starvation ensues, she perishes, while he lives on fat, and free to protect new victims of this loving kindness. If she is to be restrained, can one inferior in rectitude and continence be her keeper? It is said that beauty leans on strength; that Venus rides on a lion, now as in the old fable; but evidently the protector will despoil, unless she is armed with self-supporting and self-defending weapons.

We form societies to prevent cruelty to dumb animals, but horses and dogs are better fed and lodged, in our cities, than thousands of working women. Instead of the scythe, in the primer, we should now have the skeleton figure of Death sewing shirts. The following cases, taken at random from numberless facts reported and unreported by the press, sadly illustrate the inevitable result of denying women direct access to the sources of life and liberty:

Last evening a girl, apparently about seventeen or eighteen years of age, committed suicide by leaping into the North river from the ferry-boat James Watt. She wore a plain silk dress, with a plaid shawl and hood. For some time after the boat left the Hoboken side, she walked to and fro in the cabin, deeply agitated. Finally she sat down beside a lady, and said the cabin was very close; to another she made a similar remark, and said she had been to Hoboken to mail a letter to her friends in Germany. Greatly excited, when the boat reached the middle of the river, she rushed out, leaped over the chains, and disappeared in the water. Her body was not recovered.—*N. Y. Evening Post.*

The other day an interesting child, for she was really no more, went into the Workingwomen's Home, Franklin street, when the following dialogue occurred between her and one of the superintendents: "What is your name?" "Mary Thomson." How old are you?" "Nearly sixteen." "Where do you live?" "With my mother, in Eldridge street." "What can we do for you?" "Get me some work, please." "Where have you been working?" (Hesitatingly). "In a concert saloon." "Where?" "Corner of Chatham street and Bowery." "That's it eh? Why did you leave it?" "Well, you see, I got into a row there. Two men came in one night, and I heard them say they were going to rob a young man who was kind to me, when I told them I wouldn't let them: then, for spite, they said I stole money from them. I was taken to the Toombs, and the judge after discharging me, sent me here for work." "Where were you before going to the saloon?" "In a factory." "Why did you leave it?" "Because I only got $3 a week; my sister got the same, but it wasn't enough to support us, and we could make a great deal more as waiter girls." "How much were you paid at the saloon?" "Three dollars a week, and what we could make." "What do you mean by 'what you can make"? "Well you see, ma'am, we are allowed five cents on every drink, and then the young men treat us, and when they give us a dollar, if they are spunky and decent, they will not take back the change; besides, we get lots of jewelry, brooches, ear-rings, &c." "How much did you make a week?" "From $15 to $18, according to trade; if it was good we'd go up to $20, then down to $10. "But isn't it wicked?" (Hanging down her head). "I suppose so, ma'am; but it is hard to be hungry." "Would you like to leave the saloon?" "Yes, if I can make a living and help my poor mother." She was sent to work where she could make from $3 to $4 a week. Nothing has been heard of her since. Poor Mary! she is a good subject for some of the pity and philanthropy now going round loose in John Allen's quarters.—*New York Sun*.

One result of the religious meetings held in the dance-halls of that famous locality, was the awakening of wayward ones by the exhortations and prayers of the warm-hearted missionary. As the penitent girls stood around him in tears, ready to earn their living by better means, if permitted, he did not know what to do with his converts, who though fit for Heaven were thought unfit for society in this world, and he was obliged to confess that the religion he represented had no salvation for them here; that the boasted Christianity of the great metropolis had not heart, wit or money enough to open a way of escape from their fearful surroundings. When the women of Lyons took to suicide in great numbers, and "from no apparent cause," it was checked, as a similar mania before by the Roman Senate, by an order that the bodies of all who drowned themselves should be publicly exposed in the market place, naked. Thus was even the right to die denied by rude legislators, who thought to cure the evil, not by making life more attractive, but death more repulsive. The Welsh girl, Hester Vaughn, comes to our country in quest of relatives and work. Betrayed by a trusted protector she seeks a shelter in the solitude of the great city of brotherly love. In a lone garret in mid winter, without fire, food or friend, she gives birth to the man's child, which is found dead when she revives from the terror and agony of nearly three days' labor. Government comes not to relieve and amend, but to damn its victim to darker infamy. Execrated or ignored by self-righteous public opinion, she is arrested—tried—her last dollar taken by a lawyer for defence not made—and sentenced to be hanged. After many months' imprisonment she is pardoned by the Governor of Pennsylvania, only on condition that she will leave the country! Her "protector" is at large and votes for that Governor's re-election. In a city, known as the "heart" of the Commonwealth of Massachusetts, a young woman of intelligence, beauty, refinement, with a father, husband, brothers, uncles, able to provide material support, but unable to perceive that unliberated and unemployed energies are self-destructive, brought back to a life she loathed, and endeavored to destroy once by laudanum, walks out to the railway depot, flings herself under the wheels of a moving freight-train and is killed instantly. Like the slave-holder's jury of inquest over the body of a murdered negro, who concluded he "died of the will of God or some other disease," the coroner's verdict in this case was that she came to her death by "temporary mental aberration." Well may women assail the constituted order which assumes to restrain, rule, judge and condemn her without a hearing; for while this vicarious guardianship, with man, is conveniently impossible, to her it is a disastrous cheat. For her the prison, the scaffold, the brothel and the street; but not for her the emoluments of office, the golden prizes of business, or even a chance for an honest existence.

The drift of our social relations is from status to contract, from accepting life at second-hand to an original acquaintance with its sources. While the slave becomes citizen, and the hireling of an owner, it is a poor commentary on man's gallantry and good sense that she, whom he loves beyond all other beings incarnate, should be the last instead of the first object of this ameliorating law. The most significant spectacle of modern civilization is the trial of institutions in the court of reason, the liberation of intellect, from much which has been "bowed down to as the intention of nature and th ordinance of God." Personality, the origin and mainspring of reform, the point where renewing life enters decaying fact, is the germ of that wilderness of pronoun I's we call society, which was made for man, not man for it. When viewed from elevated points, the prominent outlooks of history, the human race, in all ages and nations, will be seen to have steadily obeyed an onward beat of things. Growth brings diversity, thinking, isms, which are to be welcomed rather than deplored, when exposed to criticism, to that prophet and law-giver of the world, free inquiry. No sensible tree rests its reputation on last year's foliage, but greets each spring with new life. That power, behind which the party of rest so often encamp—custom—favors growth, not sterility; for the tendency to advocate, the law of progress, is the perennial and overruling force of human society. Nothing is so revolutionary and convulsive, as the strain to keep things where they are, in opposition to expanding tendencies. The established government is a criticism, an amendment of a former, itself again to be revised or displaced by a larger thought. The form is less than what informs it, the temple than the deity enshrined. A violet or a cedar of Lebanon, serf, sovereign, individual being everywhere has its declaration of independence, its claim to life and scope. The all-animating impulse now bids woman "mix with action lest she wither by despair." More willing to incur responsibilities than to fulfill them, too much of man's self-government has been an effort to govern everybody except himself. The case of Sickles and Key, of Cole and Hiscox, of McFarland and Richardson, all such outbreaking evidence of the latent tragedy of domestic life, is justified on the theory of woman's incompetency to decide for herself. The husband as hereditary ruler, allowing no interference with his divine right to "protect," is self-constituted judge, jury and executioner to inflict death on any one disposed to befriend her.

Marriage is not a free civil contract, cognizant of mutually grave moral responsibilities as it should be, but a consolidated union, of which man as proposer and disposer, is supreme law. Boys are "bound out" till twenty-one; girls are bound in for life. The negro was just whose cuffy he happened to be; the wife is just whose birdie or drudge she happens to be. As masters quoted law and gospel over their slaves, so husbands emphasize their claim to wedded chattels. There is not one word in all these objections to woman's suffrage but would justify slavery or imperialism. We must therefore grant her claim, or turn our portraits of Washington and Adams to the wall, level Bunker Hill monument into the harbor, haul down the democratic republican flag and go back under king and pope. In punishing her we admit she has a moral sense to be convinced or coerced; but while conceding her the right to be hanged, we yet hold that men, eligible to the State prison and the gallows, are also eligible to Congress. Not the family, but the citizen is the social unit; for both politics and religion make individual moral being a law unto itself. Because woman is a citizen, not by the courtesy of man, but by the will of God, the fact of existence, all offensive institutions and personalities are now on trial before this fair judge.

Having shown the injustice of ruling woman without her consent, its impolicy is apparent; for what is morally wrong cannot be practically right, or innocently approved. If she has a soul, if she is a party to be consulted, her legal self-responsible equality cannot be denied, for there is no middle ground between chatteldom and freedom. The change proposed, the recognition of one half the race, hitherto ignored, is indeed momentous, though dreadful only to those who fear to do right, and trust the consequences—but forget its disastrous alternative. "The worst thing that can befall one guilty of sin, is not to be punished for it"; mindful of this fact, nature ordains her laws, more honored in the breach than the observance, to be self-executing; every evil from a civil war to a bruised finger warns us not to do so again. Enforced bondage of blacks at the South sent death to Northern homes, and those who mobbed abolitionists, by the unseen omnipotence of an idea, were hurled in embattled legions against slaveholders in the tune of "glory hallelujah." In the aberration of moral as of physical laws we get a clue to the true normal course. The festive growth of crime in those savage wilds called cities; the tragic life of women, and deadly collision of man with man; the widespread harvest of disease, deformity, insanity, degeneracy; the increasing prevalence of sexual evils before which statesmanship is baffled, religion powerless, and science dumb—these retributive results are the kindest answer nature can give to a practice which disowns divinity in its fairest human form. In the prevailing ignorance of what true affectional intercourse is, and the studied avoidance of domestic ethics both by scholars and moralists, suffrage is, of course, but the initiative, the beginning of wisdom. Women should not be too solicitous about men's sins, for they have plenty of their own to answer for. The angels we hear so much about, like men, eat, drink and catch cold, and like men, in an emergency, will lie and steal. Appealing from women to woman we aim to establish a principle, not especially to vindicate persons, and merely assert her right to opportunity and fair dealing; angel or fiend, she is entitled to work out her own salvation, to be and to do as well as to suffer.

Present practice defeats the policy it is intended to serve. To those who think women should be perpetually watched and taken care of we commend the following specimen fruit of their oriental theory fresh from China, and described in the *San Francisco Bulletin:*–

> A remarkable spectacle was the landing of the women and girls, of whom there were two hundred and forty on board. It was like landing a drove of sheep or cows. At all points of the compass were men to drive them, and they came off the boat in squads of fifteen or twenty each. The policemen and Chinese "bosses" kept each squad together and drove the entire crowd into a corner under a shed, where they stood watched as closely as ever was guarded a gang of slaves in the South. If a Chinawoman, resident here, approached too near, she ws seized and pushed away; and if any of the new comers left the crowd, she was driven back, or seized by the back of the neck and shoved to her place again. Most of those who come are young girls, many not over twelve or fifteen years of age, and nine-tenths, at least, for purposes of prostitution. Into seven or eight cars, reserved to transport them to the Chinese quarters, these creatures were driven in squads and hauled to a point on Jackson street. The women then ran the gauntlet again. The alley, which is one of the narrowest and filthiest in the city, was lined with Chinamen and women, as the strangers were driven through it, up some old rickety steps into the Dupont street theatre, and in the pit of that wretched place were again herded. Here they were assorted, marked over, and sent to the "six companies" to which they were consigned.

Men have had chief control of the world thus far, and of the results they have not much reason to be proud. For those who decline, or are denied monogamous marriage, politics, theology, science, literature, philosophy, public opinion, all the social intelligence of which history brings us an account, has evolved but three methods of solving the woman question—chattel and capital bondage, polygamy, and prostitution. Men are so much better than their laws, free instincts so often interpose to relieve victims of the "assembled wisdom," which, from State House and Congress, imposes its authoritative ignorance upon us, that many escape these sad results. But, judged by the law, and life which come out of this man-the-head-of-woman theory, it were a compliment to the male managers thereof to think society has yet no head at all. Milton being asked why a king is sometimes allowed to take his place on a throne at fourteen but not to marry until he is eighteen, replied: "Because it is easier to govern a kingdom than a woman." The poor figure men make, under the present *regime*, is the result not so much of incapacity as of attempting the impossible.

The imposing deference which, while it affects to regard woman as the pride and ornament of creation, degrades her to a toy, a cipher, fears natural order will not keep its footing, if she is allowed to go at large without keepers. But will the skeptic behind that objection please explain to us the nature of the tie which now joins, or may join him to the woman called wife? If it is force, who gave him authority to wield it! If it is fraud, the officers of justice should lay hands on him. If it is poverty, by what process did this once fascinating being, capable of infinite endeavor, become a menial in his service, dependent at his board? Is it not rather the memory of equality, of the hour when he, a glad suppliant, courted her, a free intelligence, able to accept or reject his proposals? Surrendering virgin liberty she entered his legal cage; the blooming maiden, "quickly scorned when not adored," is now the worn and faded wife, in the back-yard of his affections; and real respect for her has declined, just in proportion as she has lost the power of choice, and the control of her person. There may be men who, seeking a parlor ornament, or a subservient mistress, prefer languid helplessness to original strength in a wife; but the case of him who married the one he did, because she was the only girl in town he was not sure of before proposing, well indicates how much continent deference of the husband on the one hand, and free existence of the wife on the other, depend on her power to decline or even defy his advances. As one would rather be called a knave than a fool, so men respect woman's wickedness more than her weakness; the thorn and the bramble more than dependent vines wedded to masculine oaks. The pope said, "If we allow the right of private judgment, Protestantism may win, but Christendom will be split into sects;" Luther took the risk, and co-extensive with the prevalence of this dissolving progress of thought, the right to differ, has the believer become a law unto himself, more religious than the church. The most impressive admonition which comes to us from Jesus is, "Why even of yourselves judge ye not what is right?" The elements of order are: 1st, justice; 2d, liberty; 3d, union to repel invasion of these in any person, and which especially pledges the whole force of society to defend woman's right to decline male advances. There can be no union except between units; without keeping wedded ones always on their good behavior, as during courtship. Constantly acknowledged twoness is indispensable to coincident oneness. In urging the political question, woman brings not mere avoirdupois weight, but living mind, to be admitted to citizenship. Her enfranchisement will prove the advent of reason and conscience to politics, obedience to "law whose throne is in the bosom of God, and whose voice is the harmony of the world." The prejudice against her fulfilling any function which makes her an independent, thoughtful, self-sustaining being is excited by narrow and despotic selfishness. We have created antagonism by establishing a privileged male class.

Painful results of this effort to make two lives serve one erring will, may be seen in family quarrels, which are nature's protest against enforced coincidence. Instead of agreement, mutual deference and concord in the home, "the heart's country," we too often find hatred, conflict and chronic anarchy. These are thought to be the fault of one or both of the parties concerned, as indeed they often are, thought they generally spring from deeper causes—from coerced allegiance, ill-defined rights and duties. A Frenchman, though married, was accustomed to spend his evenings with a certain maiden lady; when his wife died, being asked why he did not marry the other, he replied that "if he did, he should not have anywhere to spend his evenings." It was remarked of another "he loved her so that one never would have thought she was his wife." An American woman brought into court, charged with pouring a pail of boiling water over a man, defended herself on the ground that she supposed it was her husband. An English wife paints her once loved lord, the courtly Bulwer, with "the head of a goat and the body of a grasshopper." Such eccentric instances are not entirely untruthful satire of the alienation which "wedded bliss" promotes when parties thereto are not free and equal factors. Approaching her before marriage with requests, afterward with commands, the lover, kneeling to an adored maid, will swear himself incapable of one of the thousand hurts he may not hesitate to inflict on her as wife. As we do not find two hills without a hollow between them, so two intelligent beings, however, loving, cannot abide together in healthful peace unless the separate, intact liberty of each is perpetually held inviolate. To commit one's self beyond recall to a finite being, for any purpose whatever, makes unitary concord impossible and undesirable. A clear-headed business man says: "The chief cause of matrimonial inharmony is in the fatal error that parties recognized in law as capable of making a contract are not also thought capable of dissolving that contract." Forced consent annihilates existing love and makes its revival impossible. Those who think liberty so dangerous an element in love would do well to, at least, imagine how the simplest affairs could proceed on the grab game their frenzied conservatism adheres to. The methods of chance, fraud and deceit, which now determine the most sacred and eventful experiences of life, would be deemed evidence of insanity if proposed as the basis of business partnership. Science, which respects aspiring insects, traverses infinite space, makes pilgrimages to the Arctic, the Amazon, the Alps and Adirondacks, studies breed in birds and herds, will ere long find it worth while to wait on women and men, and explore those dark places of the world—the kitchen, the bed-chamber, and the nursery. Matrimonial bureaus and newspaper personals, used for purposes shameful enough; the great relief a careful father feels when a daughter is well married off his hands; the scientific matchmaking; the deep-laid plans of those skillful love-brokers, mothers and maiden aunts—these indicate that business, not affection, is at the bottom of much of this romance, and make it all the more imperative on legislators to see to it that woman, in going inside the castle of law, is not disarmed and bound.

It is thought that politics will unsex her, that she will "lose her tender little ways and bashful modesties, and the bloom be rubbed off every enjoyment." This is but the revival of an old cry of tyrants, now masquerading as republicans and democrats, that the people are incapable of self-government. As an exhausted receiver defines the sphere of a rabbit suffocated under it, so imprisoning conditions within which the ages have bound woman limit her natural right to life. While men's functions and opportunities are of their own choice, women's are forced on them by circumstances. Man's duties and avocations send the soul outward; woman must always stay at home with her heart. What right has one adult citizen to forcibly determine the *status* of another? The sphere of a slave is the circle described by his driver's lash; the sphere of woman free is the realm of her heart fills, the range and height of her faculty. The ability of one marks the present sphere of that one, but leaves all space this side of God to enlarge upon. It is said that woman cannot engage in politics, or other business, because she must marry; but she is compelled to unpaid toil of many kinds, beside child-bearing, if married. Will it require more effort to go to the town hall twice than it does to attend church fifty-two times a year. Politics are merely a matter of business, the ways and means to certain ends. Principle is the what, policy is the how of affairs. The Queen of England is conceded to be, in the gentler traits, a model of her sex, though she rules an empire which encircles the globe; will our queen of hearts be less a woman when dropping a piece of paper into a box? Women in Congress, at salaries of $5,000 a year, could hardly be more damaged or damaging than as waiter girls or mistresses of those august legislators. If politics are vicious, it is high time they were cured, for "sound policy always coincides with substantial justice." The plea that women will be rudely treated by men at the polls, so far as it has any weight, only proves that male ruffians should be disfranchised; but this "chivalry objection comes about two centuries too late, for the courtesy of men has increased as the freedom of women has been accorded." If men are so bad they cannot be trusted to vote with women ought they to vote for women? Those accustomed to govern in schools, able to teach more than males can learn, will not consent to be life-long vassals of boys they educate. The mother of nine children, successfully raised and started in life, why prefer a whiff of cigar smoke to her for President? Government is a bloody, barbarous thing, chiefly because it ignores ethics of which woman is the clearer and most steadfast exponent.

> "For contemplation he and valor formed;
> For softness she and sweet attractive grace.
> He for God only; she for God and him"—

was a poet's idea, which Paul put in this presuming way: "Neither was the man created for the woman, but the woman for the man." It is because we have thus stepped between conscience and God, severed the moral law of gravitation which binds finite sovereignties to the creative centre, that our social astronomy is so sadly distracted. If the heavenly bodies are viewed as revolving around the earth, their movements appear chaotic and inexplicable; but when you reckon from the sun as center, the watch in your pocket may be timed and regulated by their exact and wondrous whirl through space. Whoso makes woman a satellite of himself is behind Copernicus in practical science; if he quote Bibles, let him listen to Jesus, who applauded a woman for *not* attending to housekeeping. If his dinner is uncooked, and his home deserted, it may be a divine voice which beckons her forth, and sordid avarice which bids her stay and grind in the prisonhouse of his selfism. By whose decree is one immortal being insphered within, and made a martyr to the private interest of another? We have no fears that, dowered with liberty, she will be less feminine, for nothing unwomanly can prevail among women. More respected in a shop or counting-room than in the kitchen, a girl acquires character and self-control in proportion as her sphere enlarges. The magnetic, thrilling touch, graceful form and movement, this animated beauty and use has laws, tendencies, and a career of its own. Superstitious bats may denounce the rising sun as a "reform against nature," for night is their day; but rose and violet welcome light and are adorned in its redeeming presence. Woman, "as God made her," we wait to see, having already too much of the man made woman. Her artificial, superinduced, enervated nature may disappear, but nature's nature will revive and prevail.

A gentle bachelor fears conscriptions of war may invade his peace if women vote, and that our fair rulers may draft for husbands. Fatally married, the wife controls one-third of his property, while he loses claim to any share in hers. He can deed nothing away without her signature, and has no use of her credit at the store, while she can buy heavily on his account, and law compels him to pay the uttermost. Withdrawing from his lordship's imperial nothingness she may levy perpetual alimony on him for a living, while he must delve to earn it, and count himself lucky to be rid of her at that. A gay creature, blushing behind her fan, outwits an elegant fop in lavender kids, who thinks all the girls dying to marry him, ensnares him in an engagement, provokes him to break it, and, in damages for breach of promise, carries off the bulk of his fortune. If this be his fate now, who can protect him when the "suppressed sex" are free, and he is obliged to risk his charms in an open market? Armed with jealousy and cunning, in the absence of better weapons of defence, ignorant, frivolous, exacting, woman now often drags man down; her subjected condition being fruitful in vices of artifice and power, of unnatural dependence, and imperious self-assertion, the aggressor, as usual, suffers most. Imbruted mind is the reflex result of the exercise of arbitrary power, and those who trample on the weak are the first to cringe to the strong. None but base natures assume to rule equals, or domineer over inferiors. We must count it, therefore, the first and chief of man's rights to undo, without asking, this injustice to woman; for in so far as he deprives her of vigor and scope does he maim himself. Alas! that any man can wish women perishing in luxurious inactivity, wedded to vice or imbecility, impaled on a needle, or starving in a garret, to be contented! Doubtless many superiors to Elizabeth Browning, Margaret Fuller, Charlotte Bronte, and George Sand are buried under our household, sewing shop, fashionable and factory life. England has one Stuart Mill, American one Emerson, but it were unlucky to have two; for why should nature be so given out as to repeat herself? In requiring woman to be the shadow, or echo of man, we mar creative intention, and rob society of the better service which intuitive sense waits to render. The value of self-supporting independence doubtless suggested the remark of a wit—"A wife is a fortune—when she is poor." As the adjective is said to be the greatest enemy of noun, though agreeing with it in gender, number and person, so woman is an adjective, an appendage of man, is useless or worse to him, and a mockery to herself, having an inalienable right to be a noun, a person accountable to infinite intelligence. Since in correcting wrong we enact right, men's actual influence will not only not be lessened, but vastly increased, by abolishing the despotic and irresponsible power they now wield. If authority is natural and beneficent, the votes of a world united cannot overthrow it; if it is usurped, the quicker it falls the better.

Fascinating weakness, "sweet irresponsibility," becomes a nullity, or hostile, when allegiance is forced, and suggests truth in an old maxim, "As many slaves, so many enemies." Since we offer a premium to adverse influence, practical sense and persuasive eloquence are turned against us; "measures which statesmen have meditated a whole year may be overturned by women in a day," and often have they conquered a nation by simply making up faces. The victims of false deference on one hand and tyrannical subjection on the other, they win through diplomatic artifice, or by sacrifices inconsistent with personal sanctity and social well-being. Impulses, which rightly directed would outflow in tenderness and rectitude, invigorate, adorn and bless mankind, now take the sexes to houses of assignation, and the very materials with which perfect society will be constructed, when the builder arrives, are added fuel to flaming heats our ignorance kindles. The "social evil," which despairing philanthropy says "no law can restrain and no power suppress," is a vast business system of supply and demand, whose natural causes and retributive results point outcasts and outcasters to the ways of healthful sanity. Not to quote Solomon and Samson, the reputed wisest and strongest of men, both of whom were conquered by women, why in Europe and America to-day are men of genius, writers, statemen and reformers, involved in family feuds, tenants of desolate homes, wanderers from what should be domestic quiet, or indulging in practices they dare not defend as right? These things cannot be dismissed with a sneer, or religiously attributed to the Prince of Evil; for the devil is only unexplained adversity, and may yet turn out to be the Deity in disguise. The old theory of natural depravity and vicarious atonement will no longer serve to darken counsel with words; for the instincts and attractions God made are not essentially unclean. Conjugal law, which in all ages and nations has "confined woman to one man, has never confined man to one woman." Virtuous Congressmen, who urge war on Mormon polygamists, should first face domestic problems at home, whose solution will require clearer heads and braver hearts than have yet appeared. In Utah husbands are responsible for their wives, required by law, at least, to provide them bread. In Boston and New York men are quite as much married, though in a clandestine and unscrupulous way. Spectacled bookworms may explore traditions of the past, grave divines declaim against laxity of morals, conceited stoics affect to be superior to fascination, but the fact remains that woman, incarnating love, has ruled and will rule man, for better for worse, just in proportion as she is assured or denied a right to herself. Not responsible to law, because unrecognized by it, she is now driven to secure recognition of her existence by depravity or rebellion. If frivolous or perverse, it is the result of false conditions; for nature has a seriously honest intent in creating a woman as in creating a man. If he makes badness a necessity and bribes to silence her moral sense, designed to call him to order, why may not the "weaker vessel" plot to upset the stronger?

Inspired by intuitive reason, this reform is also guided to its object by the light of experience. History, which is at once "a record of the past, interpretation of the present, and prophecy of the future," brings inductive evidence of what we have deduced from essential truth; that since woman is more intuitive and moral than man, her entrance into politics is guarantee of increased order and cleanliness. A few generations back literature was so obscene that an old book can hardly be trusted, without expurgation, in the hands of youth. The advent of woman as a writer swept the realm of letters clean of that infection, and made decency the first requisite of authorship. It is thought Shakespeare's elevated conception of feminine character was sensibly influenced by the fact that he wrote when Elizabeth sat upon the English throne. Be that as it may, Portia, Desdemona and Imogen heralded the sovereignty of woman on the stage, which has made the theatre a powerful auxiliary to reform. Twenty years ago many good Americans thought novel reading sinful; the appearance of "Uncle Tom's Cabin" consecrated it a pleasurable duty, set clergymen to writing stories and quickened courts and senates to memorable acts of justice. The country store, with its nightly gathering of local orators, was a scene of vulgar filth until woman stood behind the counter. The ladies' room at railroad depots, how different from the gentlemen's room, where one would suppose cattle congregate, though cattle do not need spittoons. Statistics of temperance societies show many male drunkards to one female, and the records of courts a fearful superabundance of manhood depravity. Telegraph operators stole money and profaned the wires with vile messages; when girls were put in, the receipts of cash increased and obscenity ceased. Celibate priesthoods, monkeries and nunneries have been the scandal of the church of all ages.

The precious geniuses, the beardless barbarians of colleges, "out of whom they make ministers to guide and govern us," tread under foot law, and repeal all the commandments, until girls enter to compete for the laurels of scholarship, and tame these "savage sons of God." Western colleges, to most of which both sexes are admitted, are clearly superior in moral discipline to their celibate elders of the East. Said Horace Mann of the one his name has made illustrious, "We have the most orderly, sober, diligent, exemplary institution in the country. We passed through last term, and are more than half through the present, without my having to make a single entry of any misdemeanor in our record book; not a case of any serious discipline. There is no rowdyism in the village, no nocturnal rampages making night hideous. All is quiet and peaceful; and the women of our village feel the presence of our students, when met in the streets in the evening, to be a protection rather than an exposure." Commenting on these and other facts a writer says: "Male students were first called gentlemen at Antioch." It is needless to adduce further evidence to show the right way to be the safe way. Woman's enfranchisement will renovate public affairs quite as soon as men are ready for it; and much private dirty linen is to be overhauled in the great political washing-day near at hand. With an ideal object and courage to work towards it, her arrival in literature, theatres, churches, schools or business brings reformation. As a bevy of girls were playing under my window, and one slip of womanhood put her saucy foot on a mutual right, the others scattered screaming "I'll tell mother, I'll tell mother." It seemed childish, but there was deep wisdom in the method of reconciliation, for "an ounce of mother is worth a pound of clergy," and tons of statesmen. Natural equity, whose lawgiver is love, has foreordained that the same free and equal meeting of the sexes which inspires private order and ineffable enjoyment will insure public rectitude in political action.

The recognition of woman's personality, though not regarded by any one as a cure for all evils, will be a renovating tendency, an entrance into new fields of ethics and experiences yet unexplored. Statesmen and even ministers of religion now frankly confess that they dare not voice their deepest convictions in public, but have two sets of morals, one for the closet and one for the street. Government helps reform chiefly by getting out of its way, does right from "necessity," wrong from choice; deity seems about the most impotent being known, while the devil has full swing, and wins, except here and there, when he builds his badness "up so high it topples down to the other side," and makes a sort of goodness. Judged by the records of legislation thus far, men are made of the "queerest dregs of chaos ever churned up" into sentient form. The fact that for centuries they have had representative rulers of some kind, proves that mere voting will not enact order. But the hand which denies women the ballot shuts the college and filches her earnings. Since a disfranchised class have less power of redress on account of that disability, the Labor Reform League puts her right to vote side by side with the claim of service to its reward. We thereby do not solve the labor question, but impanel a more impartial jury to try it. Not good will or votes regulate wages, but supply and demand, now generally overruled by the inequitable custom which allows one to take from another the largest possible value for the least possible return, provided he keeps out of jail. Since employers have preferred to speculate on their suffering necessities rather than concede their natural right to self-supporting independence, to equal pay for equal work with men, the few trades women have entered and mastered are so crowded that they must submit to the terms offered or surrender their places to more destitute applicants knocking at the door. We do not agree with the prevalent infidelity to right which affirms this dependence natural, and poverty of workers a "necessary evil," but summon a new judge into court—Equity. For seventy years one-eightieth part of the American people ruled our States with the iron rod of property in man; that form of political robbery is now broken, but, through subtler methods, slaveholders survive, and North and South get the earnings of labor more successfully than ever; working women, because physically the weakest, being their most deeply defrauded and helpless victims. Since one can justly take from another only what he renders an equivalent for in labor cost, the right to hold property he has not earned or received as the free bequest of others' service is purely imaginary. Interest on money, rent and profit, or dividends, are therefore inadmissible, except for work done or risk incurred; and speculative gain, in all these forms, we arraign as inherently sinful, and enforce the consequent duty of its immediate abolition. In fixing the rate of interest, Wall street, which bribes or browbeats government to do its will, fixes what proportion of earnings shall go to capital and what to labor; fixes the price of a house or calico dress, of a farm or a bunch of matches, of the largest and minutest commodity, in the remotest village of the Union. It is apparent, therefore, that the beneficent law of supply and demand has not free play, but is perverted from natural courses, and made to bring grist to the speculator's mill. A few financiers in New York and London, Paris and Berlin, controlling money, the representative of property, control the material destinies of mankind, and hold the laboring classes of all nations in wretched vassalage. The parent fraud of this gigantic system is the piratical principle that one may take from another what he does not render an equivalent for, incarnate in the government monopoly, the political usurpation which, determining by force the nature and amount of currency makes free money a penal offence. This is the first great wrong the labor movement has risen to overthrow, and, with woman's heart and vote on the right side of the battle, we are sure to win. If servant girls, plow boys and gravel tossers are with us in a moral issue, Wall street and Washington must come round. The election asks, what think ye of government? The ballot is a reply to that question, the symbol at once of opinion and power, capable of immense service to labor, peace, marriage and other reforms, though now controlled by parties who have stolen the livery of progress to serve retrogression in. Since to rule woman without her consent is tyranny, and every concession may be recalled unless the ballot forbids, we assert her right to this weapon of defence and would inscribe on the flag of authority the noble motto of St. Simon: "To each according to capacity, to all according to their work."

"But," says a gentle wife to this feminine rebellion breaking into her luxurious home, "I have all the rights I want, why come here to disturb our peace?" And the robust, tender husband, after they have spent years to construct a temple of mutual rights, thinks it a pity that like "the house which Jack built," the whole thing should tumble now. Notwithstanding the tyrannic advantage man now holds, to the honor of human nature, there are homes where he scorns to use it, where love is law, reason rules, "none command and none obey." Yet comparatively few are so fortunate in their partners as this contented wife, while vast and increasing numbers are not married, and, under existing laws, can never be. From Maine, New Hampshire, and other States; from the Canadas and beyond the seas, girls disgusted with or starved out of household service, go to factories; thence to the clothing marts of cities; thence—the path thither strewn with the diseased, the dying and the dead, such is the reluctance of nature—they crowd the swiftly descending ways of prostitution! And though the average length of life there is but four years, statistics show that the "social evil" is less destructive to woman's physical beauty and vitality than the labor system as now organized. The drift of girls (and most of these are Americans), from household and factory life to these whirlpools of vice, shows, at least, a hope of bettering their condition in that direction; and many are known to write back to their friends that they rather die there than return to what they fled from. The average life of slaves on cotton plantations was seven years, in rice fields five years; the recital of these facts roused Northern indignation and created a great political party to put down the bad thing. But our laws and customs to-day actually destroy more girls and women than slave codes murdered negroes then! How long must

American girls be crucified, on the fiery cross of self-destruction, to save this people? Does not the heart of this contented wife yearn to help us right the wrongs? Her own dear girl, left penniless and an orphan, may have to enter the struggle for life alone; will she not arm her for the conflict? Will she not save her darling boy from the savage custom of presuming to rule the one being whom he should respect as an equal?

Besides, women can afford to be indifferent to nothing which degrades women; the sad fact that "the contentment of slaves renders objection to liberty possible," makes it a more imperative duty to bestir ourselves to see justice done. Living in a world of petty details engenders narrow habits of mind, and the bounding aspirations of youth are killed out in the dull round of restricted life. "It might have been" is written over the tomb of many buried hopes. To think slavery liberty and dependence an honor; to be satisfied "with what we have rather than with what we want," that is the calamity. Speculative thought has ranged from asserting the absolute non-existence of mind, save as a form or function of matter, to a belief in the merely phenomenal existence of matter dependent on a sentient immaterial entity, mind, which, wresting from philosophy a recognition of its distinct independent being here, now comes back from the other side of death to say it lives there also. So woman from the dead level of oriental materialism, quickened by Judean religion, Grecian thought, Roman justice, German insight, and Saxon common sense, has risen to assert an original right to life. He who denies or ignores her claim must be something less than a man; while she who goes forth to proclaim it, is backed by the finest impulses of civilization, and gives new evidence of an ever-living and redeeming spiritual presence.

Our male objector who thinks it bad husbandry to harrow up wedded contentment with these exciting themes, that a strongminded woman is an intellectual tower of Pisa, under the shadow of which it were unsafe to live, forgets that domestic, like political order, rests on consent, not coercion. A large and increasing majority of applicants for divorce are women;* intelligent, sensitive natures decline proposals or accept them as a dreadful necessity to secure bread and a home; marriage is on the decline, partly for its being too expensive, but chiefly because it hinders free enterprise, and is repulsive to personal sanctity; from this one slave

*In Vermont, out of 581 divorces granted, 315 were applied for by women; in Massachusetts, out of 1,294,866; in Connecticut, out of 810,540: two-thirds of the libellants, were women. In the list of divorces granted during five years published by order of the Legislature of Massachusetts, by the side of one hundred and nineteen divorces, or separation granted for cruelty of the husband, there appear three for cruelty of the wife.—*Woolsey's Divorce and Divorce Legislation*, pp. 203, 231.

state emancipation did not reach there are more fugitives than ever fled from chattel bondage; men sound an alarm that the institution is imperilled, while women are in open revolt, or silently, patiently biding their time—such phenomena indicate deep-seated disease, whose infection spreads to every member of the body politic. Those who would send the fugitives back, tighten the laws and double the guards, are little aware of what a moral earthquake they are reading the riot act to. The old notion that slavery was the corner-stone of the republic was not more absurd and monstrous than the idea that woman's legal suppression is the corner-stone of the family. The question is not whether reform will disturb existing relations, but whether any system should continue if that system invades essential right and public interest. The simple fact that she was not consulted in framing the marriage contract, to which from the origin of society she has been forced to submit, alone justifies the woman's rights agitation; for all admit that contracts are morally binding only when parties thereto have a free voice in determining their conditions. This institution, for whose safety male keepers are so alarmed, now stands on usurped irresponsible power, and until reconstructed on the basis of equality and justice, rebellion against it is a duty. Brigham Young, who assumes woman's natural servility as a justification of his concubinal system, is consistent—giving her the ballot there is only a trick to divert attention from the settled policy to crush out all dissent by orthodox violence—but monogamist objectors seem unaware that she must go back to polygamy, or forward to liberty. One cannot always remain suspended between something and nothing. To say the wife "belongs" to the husband, or the husband to the wife, implies ownership and calls for the deed of purchase. In denying her equality he herds her with brutes; claims himself to be a freeman, but insists that she shall live under rude codes of the dark ages. He lives in the nineteenth century, she in the ninth, and he puts a thousand years between himself and his lady-love in disfranchising her. We do not make love by statute and cannot unmake it that way. The law of cohesion between souls is as natural and inevitable as between atoms and globes. The fascinating intelligence at whose feet, in his truest moment, the male lover lays all; the qualities of devotion, fortitude, self-sacrifice all bow to, in the gravest epochs of life—at the altar, the cradle and the tomb—will assert a regulating control if allowed free play. The true nuptial knot is in the heart, not on the house top. In drawing-room or convention, nursery or senate, sewing circle or market-place, it matters little where thought ranges if light spreads and souls are born again.

What is apparent in the outer, material phases of life man inhabits, is so much more deeply true of its inner, spiritual realms, native to woman, that her emancipation will prove, not a source of discord, but the beginning of agreement. Had the wits of sham conservatives aimed at extreme badness, they could not have invented a scheme more fruitful, in conflict and immorality, than the present *regime*. The grave apprehensions of stately editors and divines, who think it unsafe to break every yoke, and obey good rather than evil, like the anxiety of slave masters for the results of negro liberty, whould be more noteworthy if they had the merit of disinterested intelligence. So far are we from ignoring the potential force of the sexual passions, or undervaluing the claims of maternity and offspring, that the originators of the woman's rights reform were the first to give those themes serious and intelligent consideration. Since this question touches the quick of life, goes to the foundations of order and being; precisely because its subject is woman, not a weak man, because the tragedy of motherhood is fraught with momentous interests to herself and the race, must she have free right to live and move independent of finite dictation. The maternal instinct is impaired by the very method now frantically clung to. Statistics prove that fœticide is not generally induced by pressure on the means of subsistence, but rather originates in causes attendant on dainty care-taking and luxury. Domestic animals often kill and devour their young; petted hens while sitting chip and eat their eggs. Child-murder is comparatively rare in poor countries like Ireland and among laboring people of all nations; while in Paris and New York, by the "upper" classes, it is increasingly practiced; mothers often provoking abortion to preserve their physical beauty, and escape from the "home sphere" into the delirious whirl of fashionable life. Dr. Storer shows* that the practice of abortion, by the American women of Massachusetts and New York, is so limiting the increase of population that it is maintained chiefly by foreign immigration. The number and the successes of abortionists is notorious; hardly a newspaper that does not contain their open and printed advertisements, or a drug store whose shelves are not crowded with nostrums publicly and unblushingly displayed. The feminine instinct of these "womanly" women—not strong-minded, and never seen in suffrage conventions—is so perverted that they seem unconscious of the crime to themselves and society they are guilty of; and in selfish egotism rival even those of the most luxurious cities of Europe and Asia, who, subsisting on fugitive attachments, find in marriage a convenient screen behind which to shelter their indiscretions. Our critics must cease this wise nonsense which says to woman "Be Good," and makes

*"Why Not"? and "Criminal Abortion in America." See also in M. Huc's "Journey Through the Chinese Empire," vol. II., page 327, the shocking prevalence of infanticide where the subjection of women is reduced to a system.

man the sample piece of what she is to copy from. It is high time that the one most deeply interested in marriage and reproduction should be consulted as a responsible partner; that the maker of men should have free choice of materials, methods and conditions wherewith to perfect her wondrous work.

Educating her for service, not for show, pleasure or sacrifice merely, we must first aim to make a woman, of whom the wife and mother will be, more important, complete and attractive attributes than hitherto. But education, which should develop strength, not cripple it, has been to her, thus far, perversion. As man is trained to get money she is trained to get married, adorned or distorted to suit the whims of a destined master. If nature rebels she is damned to living burial as an "abandoned woman," an "old maid"; if devoted, "constant," she has the honor to expire in flames of lust on the funeral pyre of a husband morally dead though physically living. Nothing can exceed the presumption, the devilish criminality, of such wretches as Sickles and McFarland who, because they "love her," deliberately murder a wife's friend on the ground that to give her aid and comfort is an "overt act" of treason to marriage. Her natural right to be a mother or anything else, unless she first gets herself a legal dictator, is yet to be conceded. But neither the tyranny of law nor the merciless grasp of marital "rights" will prevail against the steady advance of woman to equality and fair play. "He that sitteth in the heavens shall laugh, the Lord shall have them in derision"; governments, nations, races perish, but liberty and love are immortal. The affection of the sexes for each other, of parents for children, new every morning, fresh every evening, and repeated every moment, over-rules all other human forces, defies all intrusive impertinence, and will outlive all legislative dictation. The spiritual life which overflows and interfuses these tenements of clay, now and forever, waits to ennoble the most forlorn outcast if she will but believe and strive. Woman is woman because tenderness, reason, love, intuition, beauty, the truly feminine qualities, flow direct from infinite sources, and are not reservoired exclusively in any male protector. Pecuniary not less than political justice must be granted, for men cannot share the privileges of free, honorable love until they cease to steal. Marriage, not the subject under discussion, is foreign to the purpose of this essay; it will come up in due time, but sufficient unto the day is the good thereof. It is desired now only to affirm woman's natural, inalienable claim to that principle of common law, everywhere conceded to man, which holds all persons innocent until proved guilty; to share in the serviceable government which lifts up the oppressed, in pulling down oppressors, and finds its chief guarantee in popular freedom, and the imperishable sense of right.

Who says democracy will not justify itself in her as in him? If the Goddess of Liberty is worthy of the imperial honor of a statue on the dome of the Federal Capitol, she may enter ward rooms and town halls as a voter. When the mailed hand of force is withdrawn, leaving woman free like man to do wrong even at her own cost, to stand or fall on her own merits, she will do well—in making love or laws, a loaf of bread or an immortal being—just in proportion as responsibility is recognized, intelligence enlarged and liberty inviolate. All hail, Equality! Then indeed will moral regeneration begin, and social concord be possible, when the sexes, meeting as intelligent beings, mutually accountable to each other and to destiny, engaged irretrievably to nothing but right, reason together on the issues of life, and welcome its yet untried privileges.

The male

"Has no more subtle master under Heaven
Than is the maiden passion for a maid;
Not only to keep down the base in him,
But teach high thought and amiable words,
And courtliness and the desire of fame,
And love of truth and all that makes a man."

Woman has no better friends incarnate than men whom she can freely love, respect and trust; and no worse enemy than him who, for any purpose whatever, would subordinate her being to his. Liberated, self-loyal womanhood is to be the connecting link between isolation and society, the "guardian angel of our associated destiny." Both sexes need to be profoundly converted to truth and honor; for liberty is not the goddess we read of, but male, incontinent, libertine when not overruled by an intelligent moral sense. Rights obtained should impel to corresponding duties; and free, intelligent inter dependence making love relations less formal and promiscuous, but more select, intimate and refining. Each belongs to self and others, one being only half man without woman, and the other only half woman without man. The family retains its place, in the hope of unity and honesty, at least in a narrow circle; enlightened liberty will eliminate its defects and universalize its merits. As the old spinning-wheel and power loom have given place to great factories; so the single tenement, with its cooking drudgery, washtubs and neglected children, will disappear in reorganized housekeeping, the scientific classification of woman's industrial and maternal functions. Be just and fear not; what love has joined, can be put asunder only by destroying the conditions out of which love springs and flourishes. Whether marriage is induced by affinity of likes or unlikes, the subtle attraction of essential worth and beauty, the fascination of form and touch, the base allurement of money, tyranny of circumstances, or carnal coalition from mere proximity; whether society rests on a combination of opposing or concurrent forces, everything good is to be gained, and nothing but bad lost, in the new departure involved in woman's enfranchisement.

That it will bring revolutionary and startling changes is evident; but, knowing in whom and what they have believed, new seas of agitation, however tempestuous, have no perils to those who sail by the compass of right. In the conflict of thought with idolatry, feudalism, priestcraft, political and chattel slaveholders, the hearts of strong men often failed them for fear; yet, impelled by the inward might of faith, through ignorance, superstition, avarice, infidelity and cowardice, the moral sense steadily gropes its way toward order, system, empire. The same law which holds ocean in its bed and planets in their courses will inspire these two mysterious sovereignties we call man and woman to transact their gayest and gravest affairs, with no jar or hurt, but mutual assistance to each other, and the general welfare. That widely looked-for personage, yet to rise from this agitation, like Venus from surf of the Grecian sea, the coming woman, no feminine man or masculine opposite, with greater physical vigor of finer fibre, will bring impressive beauty, melting tenderness, ethereal grace, mental force, moral rectitude, such as the exhaustless sources of being yearn to incarnate. That passion now thought incapable of analysis, uncertain in its origin, accidental in its course, inspiring alike the darkest and brightest experiences, replete with ecstasy and tragedy, love, inherently pure, ineffably beneficent, is destined to make inclination one with duty, liberty the bride of order, and justice the security of citizens and the life of states.

EZRA H. HEYWOOD

UNCIVIL LIBERTY:

AN ESSAY

TO SHOW

THE INJUSTICE AND IMPOLICY OF RULING

WOMAN

WITHOUT HER CONSENT.

BY E. H. HEYWOOD,

AUTHOR OF "YOURS OR MINE," "THE LABOR PARTY," "CLOSET AND STREET," "THE GOOD OF EVIL," "WAR METHODS OF PEACE," "INNER LIFE," "THE CHURCH," "SOCIAL JUSTICE," AND OTHER ADDRESSES.

SIXTIETH THOUSAND.

PRINCETON, MASS.:
COÖPERATIVE PUBLISHING COMPANY.
1873.

WORCESTER: PRINTED BY CHAS. HAMILTON.

Facsimile of the cover of the original 1873 edition of UNCIVIL LIBERTY.